FATHER LOUIE

FATHER LOUIE

Photographs of Thomas Merton

 by Ralph Eugene Meatyard

WITH AN ESSAY BY GUY DAVENPORT

EDITED BY BARRY MAGID

TIMKEN PUBLISHERS

Ralph Eugene Meatyard, photograph by Thomas Merton

The photographs of Thomas Merton reproduced in this book have been printed from Ralph Eugene Meatyard's original negatives by his son, Christopher. He has re-created exactly the size, format, tonality, and contrast of the original vintage prints. Meatyard never made proof prints, but instead examined his negatives directly and usually printed about one out of every three. In the case of the Merton negatives the ratio was higher: he printed about half. He generally made only one print from a negative, occasionally two or three. One negative, however, he printed nine times (page 101), probably because Merton died soon after the photograph was taken. Three images in this book (pages 13, 37, 103) are from negatives never printed by Meatyard.

The photographs of Meatyard by Merton, reproduced on the opposite page and page 105 were kindly loaned by the Thomas Merton Studies Center at Bellarmine College in Louisville, Kentucky. The director of the Center, Dr. Robert E. Daggy, transcribed much of the correspondence between Meatyard and Merton. The Merton Legacy Trust and Ralph Eugene Meatyard's family graciously granted permission to publish the letters and reminiscences. Excerpts from Merton's *Cables to the Ace* (© 1968 The Abbey of Gethsemani, Inc.) are reprinted by permission of New Directions Publishing Corporation.

Copyright © 1991 Timken Publishers, Inc.,
225 Lafayette Street, New York, NY 10012
Photographs by Ralph Eugene Meatyard copyright © 1991,
by the Estate of Ralph Eugene Meatyard

Library of Congress Cataloging-in-Publication Data

Meatyard, Ralph Eugene, 1925–1972.
    Father Louie : photographs of Thomas Merton / by Ralph Eugene
  Meatyard ; with an essay by Guy Davenport.
       p.   cm.
    ISBN 0-943221-09-9
    ISBN 0-943221-10-2 (pbk.)
    1.   Merton, Thomas, 1915–1968.   2.   Merton, Thomas,
1915–1968—Pictorial works.   3.   Merton, Thomas, 1915–1968—
Correspondence.   4.   Meatyard, Ralph Eugene, 1925–1972—
Correspondence.
I.   Davenport, Guy.   II.   Title.
BX4705.M542M36   1991
271'.12502—dc20   90-21430
                                                 CIP

CONTENTS

PREFACE

by Barry Magid

By entering the monastery, a monk dies to the world and to his former identity, beginning a new life in Christ and receiving a new name. Thus Thomas Merton became Father Louis to the brethren of Our Lady of Gethsemani.

To the world, which continued to receive his books, he remained Thomas Merton, best-selling author and spiritual guide to his and our generation. But Merton was acutely aware of the danger of being trapped by these personae, and already in *The Seven Storey Mountain* he refers to *that* Thomas Merton as "my double, my shadow, my enemy." To asceticism and obedience, the traditional monastic antidotes for egotism, he added his own self-deprecating humor and a refusal to take his own importance or achievement too seriously. Always one to delight in playful pseudonyms—a letter to the editor of *Jubilee* was signed "Marco J. Frisbee"—Thomas Merton, who disappeared into Father M. Louis, O.C.S.O., emerged in his later years simply as "Louie," as he signed himself in his last letter home from Asia.

Gene Meatyard's photographs, with their use of chance, motion, and multiple exposures, mirror the ever-changing, ephemeral nature of the Self, which we normally fool ourselves into imagining as fixed and stable. When we open a book of photographic portraits, we are used to looking for how the photographer has captured the essence of his subject in a given image.

These pictures don't do that.

The quotations are from *A Vow of Conversation* (Farrar, Straus & Giroux, 1988) and *The Seven Storey Mountain* (Harcourt, Brace, 1948).

Rather than gratify what Merton called "the hunger of having a clear satisfying idea of *who* he is and *what* he is and where he stands," they subvert the whole notion of Essence, or of a Self to be captured. While some of the photographs tantalize us by catching Merton in what we imagine to be an especially revealing or even "spiritual" moment, others offer a blur, an awkward or even apparently unexpressive scene. Taken together, they present the lesson that Merton, like all of us, like any moment, cannot be grasped or fixed by an image, whether photographic or mental.

Anything you can grasp is not it.

Go after the Essence and you'll just come up with another moment's mask. (Ask Lucybelle Crater.)

Who was Gene Meatyard, or Thomas Merton, or Louie?

I don't know.

Their shared genius was to defy definition, to remain a blur, unpredictably and mysteriously alive. But don't think there was anything special about them.

Emptied of the pursuit of specialness, we receive the grace of ordinary life, "as if existence itself were heavenliness."

Early winter 1967, meal—cheese, bread, wine, talk 3 hours

Early winter 1967, Merton talks with Jonathan Williams and Guy Davenport in his cabin, icons on wall

Early winter 1967, reading from Notes for *Cables to the Ace*, then called "Edifying Cables"

Early winter 1967, by favorite place at monks' sheep barn, many poems written here

TOM AND GENE

by Guy Davenport

Ralph Eugene Meatyard met Thomas Merton on January 17, 1967, at the Trappist monastery of Our Lady of Gethsemani near Bardstown, Kentucky. The day was bright and cold. The next day Merton wrote his friend Bob Lax that he had been visited by "three kings from Lexington," as Michael Mott records in his biography. Tom's letters to Lax were always madcap and full of private jokes, so that why we were cast as the Magi must remain a mystery. We brought no gifts, we came in Gene's car, but we were decidedly remote in religion: Gene, I think, was a lapsed Methodist; Jonathan Williams, a very lapsed Episcopalian; and I, a Baptist who would figure in Tom's judgment as the only real pagan he had ever met.

Tom was grateful that we weren't pious. His life was bedeviled by people who had read a third of *The Seven Storey Mountain* and wanted to say they had met him. Just why we made our visit I'm not certain. Jonathan Williams was well into his ongoing enterprise of meeting every person worth knowing on the face of the earth, and had remarked that he "had no sense of Merton the man" and wanted to look in on him. Jonathan was at the time on a weeklong visit at my house, showing slides and giving readings at the University of Kentucky. Some years before, he had introduced me to Gene Meatyard, optometrist and photographer. Gene and I had become friends, and I had begun urging him to photograph literary figures. Eventually he photographed Louis Zukofsky, Wendell Berry, James Baker Hall, Jonathan Greene, Hugh Kenner, among others. It was therefore as a portraitist that he was along. I was there because Tom had read my poem *Flowers and Leaves* (to his fellow monks, at table, moreover;

the silent Trappists may hear secular writing while they eat, and it was one of Tom's chores to read to them).

This frosty January day has become magic in my memory. Merton met us at the lodge. He was dressed in dungarees, sweater, and hooded jacket. He looked like a cross between Picasso and Jean Genet. He got into Gene's car, to guide us to his cement-block one-room cabin in the woods in back of the abbey. Tom had just before this become a desert father, the first in a thousand years. He remarked wryly that the abbot suspected him of having orgies there (Joan Baez had been a visitor a short time before, against all rules: two signs along the approach to Gethsemani warned away the female sex—the first read NO LADIES PERMITTED, the second NO WOMEN). Tom and the abbot had had disagreements about the rules for a desert father, especially about Tom's growing habit of visiting people in Louisville and Lexington. "Who's to say," Tom countered, "if Saint Anthony didn't take the streetcar into Alexandria when he'd had it with his loneliness?"

The hermit's cabin had its bed zoned from the rest of the inside by a Mexican blanket. We got to see the bed—Spartan to be sure—when Tom reached under it to bring out a half-bottle of the local bourbon. There was an oil stove, for heat, as well as a handsome fireplace. A few sacred icons, all folk art, were on the walls. The books were largely poetry. I noted letters on his desk from Marguerite Yourcenar and Nicanor Parra. Tom Merton knew no strangers; we settled in to good talk, as if we had known each other for years.

Gene had begun the conversation as we got out of the car. His incredibly sharp eyes had seen a rock by a pine tree near the cabin porch, and he remarked casually that it had been photographed by someone and used on the cover of a New Directions book. Tom had taken the picture. So Gene and Tom first met as fellow photographers. And it is not every day you meet someone who can identify from a phenomenal visual memory a rock among rocks and a pine among pines. (I once needed Gene to identify a man in his thirties of whom I had only a photograph at age ten. This was at an airport; Gene identified him as he emerged from the plane.)

My notes say that at some point Tom did a dance, which he said was Chilean, although I now cannot remember any music or Tom dancing. He made drawings for us by dipping weeds in ink and slapping them onto a sheet of typing paper. He drew a horse, very Zen in its strokes. We had arrived at eleven, having been lost for an hour on back Kentucky roads; the matter of lunch arose. Tom served us goat cheese made at the abbey, packets of salted peanuts, and jiggers of bourbon. Jonathan asked at this Epicurean meal what Tom was writing. He was writing what came to be Section 35 of *Cables to the Ace*. Would we like to hear some of it?

He read: "C'est l'heure des chars fondus dans le noir de la cité. Dans les caves, les voix sourdes des taureaux mal rêvés! l'océan monte dans les couloirs de l'oeil jusqu'à la lumière des matins: et ils sont là, tous les deux: le Soleil et le Franc-Tireur."

My notes say: Gene photographed as we talked. For the rest of their friendship, up until Tom's departure for the East, Gene photographed.

Tom's bladder needed frequent relief. The outhouse was the home of a black snake. Tom instructed us, if we wanted to use this amenity, to kick the door first and shout, "Get out, you bastard!" In the afternoon we walked up the hill to the reservoir—the Monks Pond of Tom's magazine—and it was on this walk that he talked about *Flowers and Leaves* and suggested that Jonathan consider becoming a Trappist. In the pond, he said, there was nude bathing in the summer, for those so minded, and he remembered swimming there with the Stephen Spenders.

My notes say: A warm, generous, frank, and utterly friendly man.

We left at four, having been given bread from the refectory and introduced to Brother Richard, who, clerking in the abbey's cheese shop, was allowed to talk.

When Bonnie Jean Cox later met Tom, she whispered to me, "This is not the man who wrote *The Seven Storey Mountain*," as indeed he wasn't. It was Bonnie's observation, when we heard of Tom's death in Bangkok, that he had held out his hand to God on his arrival in heaven and hooted, "Hello, you old son of a bitch!"

Tom's reputation was already myth in these last two years of his life, when Gene Meatyard was one of his closest friends. Gene, merriest of men and with a wicked sense of humor, delighted in my telling him that I had been to an English department cocktail party where some visiting scholar was impressing us with his inside dope about Father Marie Louis, Order of the Cistercians of the Strict Observance. Did we know—few did—this English prof asked us in awed tones, that Merton had retreated from the monastery, incredibly disciplined as it was (sign language only, vigils at the altar through the night, incessant prayer and unremitting study), for a bare hut in a Kentucky forest, where he'd grown a long beard, and where absolutely no one saw him? He communicated only with God.

This professor was enjoying himself immensely, imparting privileged information to the ignorant.

At an opportune moment, I said, watching the ghastly look that grew on his face:

"Tom Merton was by the house day before yesterday, turning up on my porch after a phone call from the bus station. He was in mufti: tobacco-farmer field clothes, with a tractor cap. He made quite a dint in my bottle of Jack Daniel's, and was excited to find that I had a text of Bernardus Silvestris's *De mundi universitate*, about which we had a lively discussion. We also talked about Buster Keaton and the superiority in comic genius of the silent film over the talkies, Charles Babbage, French painting, and Lord knows what else, including Catalan, a dictionary of which he'd hoped I could lend him."

It was quite clear that the professor took me to be not only a fool but a jackanapes, and soon after this I was told that one of my department who listened to this drivel reported me to the administration as a fraud. (I had just come to the university, and was suspect for various other reasons.)

I am sorry that I could not have recounted a later appearance of Tom in Lexington, when he, Gene, an editor of *Fortune* and Columbia classmate of Tom's, and I went to lunch at the Ramada Inn. The editor of *Fortune* had rented a car at the airport, wrecked it, and had minor cuts and bruises, enough to have bloodied his clothes. He sported a bandage around his head, and invited second looks. Gene was in a neat business suit. Tom was, as before, dressed as a tobacco farmer. The four of us were served with the utmost courtesy, beginning with martinis, which Tom downed four of. One of Tom's topics at this meal was the architecture of Buddhist temples.

It is my guess that Tom was, like Saint Paul, all things to all men. The pious monk of the professor at the cocktail party certainly existed. He was indeed the vigilant before the altar in the cold watches of a winter's night. He was also the man who asked Joan Baez to take off her shoes, as he hadn't seen a woman's foot in years. He showed me where she'd danced in the wheatfield for him, barefoot and singing. He had a healthy distrust of the trendy and velleitous in religion. He winced when pious visitors from the world hunted him down. One Sunday afternoon he, Gene, Bonnie, and I walked to the remotest part of a field, in hiding from the inevitable elbow swingers. "Even so," he said, "it was here that a car stopped, and a family got out, and before I could get away they held up their infant son dressed in a Trappist habit." It was this same afternoon that we learned Tom gave lectures to the abbey on Eastern religions. He'd looked at his watch, said, "Damn! I have to jackrabbit over to the big house and do the Sufis," and trotted off at a lively pace, shouting that he'd be back in fifty minutes.

Gene Meatyard was at this time deep into Zen, which he saw as a philosophy relevant to his art as well as his life. Zen was, however, but one of many of Gene's concerns. He was, when he met Tom Merton, one of the most distinguished of American photographers, all the more distinguished and typically American for being invisible in a Kentucky university town. He was known to the members of the Lexington Camera Club, which was, with Van Deren Coke, Guy Mendes, James Baker Hall, and Robert C. May among its members, one of the epicenters of American photography. He had a large circle, or circles, of friends. Born in 1925 in

Normal, Illinois (he treasured that name), he invented himself. He was deeply, eclectically, educated, despite a typical high school and Williams College. When he met Tom Merton he was married to the charming and beautiful Madeleine ("Mattie") and had three children, Mike, Chris, and Melissa. Their home, which Tom visited frequently, was as friendly and comfortable a place as a home can be. While it bore the stamp of all of the Meatyards' hobbies, Gene's hand was everywhere—his objet-trouvé sculptures, his collection of rare recordings of jazz, his books and photographs.

The laughable was Gene's passion. He had a notebook full of peculiar names which led, in time, to the idea of Lucybelle Crater and her daughter Lucybelle Crater (a misremembering of Flannery O'Connor's Lucynelle Crater and her daughter Lucynelle Crater). One of Lexington's citizens at the time was Carlos Toadvine, whose stage name was Little Enis. Gene was fascinated with his own name, Meatyard, and was delighted when I pointed out that it is the Middle English *meteyeard*, or yardstick, cognate with the name Dreyfus. And that his first name is properly pronounced "Rafe." He approved of Edward Muggeridge's changing his name to Eadweard Muybridge.

My first response to Gene's photographs was to see them as images parallel to Henry James's evocation of hallucinations—the blurred, half-recognizable face in the shadows. I did not know at the time that Gene had worked in many styles, that he had made documentary studies as brilliant as Margaret Bourke-White's and had begun as a fairly traditional modernist, echoing Minor White and Charles Sheeler. All the Merton portraits belong to a period of experimentation in which Gene was exploring his own mastery of the camera. He would take pictures seemingly offhandedly, without looking in the viewer. There was an afternoon of talk with Tom, at Gene's house, in which he took some amazing photographs all but secretly. I was aware that the camera was there, on its tripod, and that Gene fiddled with it from time to time.

There were also elaborate stagings and poses. There was an afternoon when Gene took Tom and me to an abandoned farm, stood us under a clothesline, had us peer into a rain barrel, posed us back to back, like duelists. This was at the time that the Anglican bishop James Pike had wandered off into a desert in the Southwest and the papers were full of speculation as to his whereabouts. "All bishops are mad," Tom offered.

When Edward Rice's *The Man in the Sycamore Tree: The Good Times and Hard Life of Thomas Merton* was published in 1970, Gene read it with care and a great deal of skepticism. This was the first exposure of Merton as a thoroughly human, frequently confused, complex of personalities. The Merton who emerges from Michael Mott's sensitive, thorough, and uncompromisingly honest biography of 1984, *The Seven Mountains of Thomas Merton*, is a turbulence of conflicting directions. He was a hermit committed to silence, meditation, and solitude, who was one of the most gregarious of human beings. His vow of chastity had to contend with an uncontrollable desire to be in love and to be loved. In the 1960s he was very much like an adolescent just discovering sex. In religion he sometimes seemed more a Sufi and Buddhist than a Christian. His poetry at this time made a quantum leap into a highly charged style derived from Nicanor Parra and a new vision of absurdity.

Gene Meatyard certainly contributed to this existentialist view of the world. He had made a kind of surreal poetry of the visual.

Gene's Lucybelle Crater series—couples wearing the same masks in every picture, one a transparent mask which aged the subject, the other a grotesque Halloween witch's face—is contemporary with *Cables to the Ace* and *The Geography of Lograire*. Gene was interested in what happens to the rest of the body when the face is masked. A mask, like an expression, changes the way we see feet and hands, stance and personality. These photographs are both satiric and comic; their insight, however, is deep. We are all masked by convention and pretense. Merton would have said that we are masked by illusion. He was, as Gene perceived, a man of costumes (masks for the whole person). His proper costume was a Cistercian robe, in which he looked like a figure out of El Greco or Zurbarán. He liked wearing this in the wrong place, a picnic, for instance, of which Gene made a set of photographs. This was one of Gene's favorite modes: the candid shot of families and groups, a use of the camera as old as photography, but in Gene's masterly hands a psychological sketchbook, and a comedy of manners.

The breakthrough in Tom's poetry came from a convergence of forces: reading Flannery O'Connor (whose stories are Christian mimes in a comic vernacular), *Mad* magazine, and the ads in *The New Yorker*, and a vision from the Cargo Cults of New Guinea. The *New Yorker* ads seemed to Tom to disclose the true sickness of our time. They are chic and unobjectionable, and yet they are as vivid a temptation of Saint Anthony as any painted by Bosch or Brueghel. They present, masked, what *Mad* openly and jeeringly exposed. The New Guinea Cargo Cults were expectations by primitive people that the American army would someday return with the same kind of wonderments (airplanes, canned food, whiskey, recorded music, magic medicine and skilled surgeons, bombs and rifles, boots and metal hats) they had brought in the Second World War.

Is not modern Christianity, Tom asked in his poetry and in his inmost meditations, our Cargo Cult? Physical desire, as any Buddhist knows, is insatiable. It has no plateau of satisfaction, it offers no rest at all. The family with one automobile wants two; the family with two, three. Wealth has become not advantage and pleasure in the world, but a hunger for more wealth. Thus all sense of measure, of inner peace, becomes impossible.

Both Gene and Tom had evolved a personal discipline which they associated with Zen—self-mastery as well as mastery over adversity. Tom at this time was in correspondence with hundreds and was maintaining friendships of varying intensity (from deep love to casual interest); he was reading in the literatures of both sides of the world; he was practicing the severe discipline of being a desert father. He wrote a phenomenal number of pages in these years: a *Lives of the Saints* that still lies in the vaults of the Vatican, unpublished; *Confessions of a Guilty Bystander*; journals, letters, poems. (Every monk in a Trappist community has his work; Tom's was writing.) Each friend—psychiatrist, publisher (James Laughlin, of New Directions, who was a worldly confessor for Tom's very worldly sins, literary advisor, and emissary between Tom and the literary establishment), typists, devoted conspirators and runners of errands, even suppliers of money for phone calls and drink (this kitty was known as the Mars Bar Fund, all contributions welcome), Islamic theologians, and on and on—interacted with a different concern of Thomas Merton's complicated roundness.

In Gene Meatyard he must have seen, at first, a photographer and a quiet ironist. Later, I think, he saw something like his opposite: a man happily married, with children, a profession, and an art. Such complementarity is rare. Gene, whether making chocolate for Christmas gifts—chocolate as eaten by archangels, powers, and dominions—or violet jam, did everything in the best way possible. He had combined the two ways of making people see better, optometry and photography. He had perfect manners; he was intelligent, responsive, and good-natured. And like Tom, he could deplore and delight in the absurdity of things. Gene, who normally drove and read at the same time, could rejoice in coming upon a Lexington driver who was technically blind, with a license from the police that restricted his driving to less traveled streets. "*Mais bien sûr!*" was Tom's approval of both of these apparent absurdities.

The relationship of artist and model is one that has taken its place as a subject in art at least since Vermeer. Picasso meditated on it in many suites of drawings and etchings; it is implicit throughout Rembrandt. In our time artist and subject have an equal claim on our attention. When Henri Cartier-Bresson photographed the old

Matisse, the result is "a Cartier-Bresson," the subject of which is Matisse. All of Gene's photographs of Tom Merton are "Ralph Eugene Meatyards," subject: Thomas Merton.

Gene's studies of the Zukofskys, Louis and Celia, achieved in their New York apartment, are also very much "Meatyards." They had met Gene here in Lexington, at my house, and knew his work, and knew what they were in for. Gene liked to say that he photographed essence, not fact. Gene read Zukofsky before he photographed him; Zukofsky's layered text turns up as double exposures in the portraits, as oblique tilts of the head, as blurred outlines. The "innocent eye" of Monet and Wallace Stevens was not for Gene: he needed to know all he could about his subjects. He did not, for example, know enough about Parker Tyler, who sat for him, and came out as a complacent southern gentleman on a sofa, and the photograph is neither Parker Tyler nor a Meatyard.

The first thing we notice about Gene's portraits of Tom is the wild diversity. Here's Tom playing drums, and Tom the monk, and Tom the tobacco farmer, and Tom the poet (holding Jonathan Williams's thyrsus). Many were taken when Tom could not have been aware that he was being photographed. Many are posed in a collaboration between artist and subject.

Gene had agreed with me that Tom could look eerily like Jean Genet—John Jennet, as Gene pronounced the name, with typical Meatyardian intrepidity. This was within the psychological game of belying appearances, one of Gene's games. For Tom resembled the French outlaw and prose stylist only when he was in his farmer's clothes; that is, in a mask for the body. (Gene had no interest in the nude, and I know of only one such photograph, made for a show of the naked body; Gene predictably photographed his subject in a bathroom, where nudity is normal and necessary, and chose for his model the shyest and most modest of his friends, the poet Jonathan Greene.)

One of Gene's unachieved projects was to make photographs to illustrate William

Carlos Williams's *Paterson*, a work he found endlessly interesting. By this time Gene had already started going wide afield to photograph portrait subjects, and I assumed that he was off to Paterson, New Jersey. "Oh, no," Gene said, "I'll do the photographs here, in Lexington." This is worth knowing, and Williams would have gasped at the originality of the perception, at a fellow artist who saw the truth of his poem as a universal myth. A Dutch Madonna of the sixteenth century is a Dutch girl with a Dutch baby on her lap. What Williams wrote about Paterson must be true of Lexington, and Gene's pictures would have been a commentary on *Paterson* at the highest critical level: parallel creation.

Tom Merton has been, and will be, written about extensively. He was photographed as much as the pope. We will always be reinterpreting Merton the man, with all his divergent energies, along with Merton the theologian, moralist, and philosopher. A photographic record is so obviously prime material for the biographer and commentator that we forget its importance, because of its usualness in our time. Try to imagine an image of Jesus, drawn or painted from life, and the kind of writing it would generate. Consider the mythic charisma Lincoln's photographs have contributed to our sense of him. We are all healthily aware that photographs lie, deceive, and misrepresent, and yet we go right on reading them as if they were expert witnesses. Richard Nixon's unfortunate face seems to spell out his lack of character, his villainy, his deviousness. "The body," said Wittgenstein, "is a picture of the soul."

Another distinguished American photographer, Douglas Haynes, of Arkansas, photographs children only, and has a thousand tricks of gesture and voice for beguiling his subjects into the maskless natural innocence he's a master of capturing. A photographer of animals has the same problem, for a photograph is a stage, the subject an actor, and the moment of exposure a cue. Gene had no studio, never directed his subjects, and usually looked away, as if uninterested, before he triggered the shutter. I have spent several days being photographed by Gene, and never knew when he was photographing. We kept a conversation going, usually an exchange of

33

anecdotes. I knew, however, where Gene's eyes were: they were on light, on shadows. A Meatyard photograph is always primarily an intricate symmetry of light and shadow. He liked deep shadows of considerable weight, and he liked light that was decisive and clean.

He liked resistant structures. Many of Gene's photographs are of buildings, especially interiors, in the process of demolition, or of buildings holding up under time. Time itself may have been his ultimate subject, what it does to people and the world. The Lucybelle Crater sequence is of people momentarily aged forty years by masks. His own triumphant portrait, by Guy Mendes, is of him waving good-bye with his hat, as if being seen off on a train.

Gene was, at least after a year of knowing Merton, conscious of photographing a figure who was undergoing a transition. There were rumors that Merton was going to stay in the East, probably as a Zen monk in Japan. ("Not Tom!" Gene said. "Not him!") There was the sense that something had to give: that Tom was being torn by the world and the Church, by his genuine desire for total solitude and his equally genuine passion for people, for talk. He wanted Christianity to be refound, and the Church was edgily afraid of him. He was a new thing in Catholicism: a truly ecumenical spirit. When he wrote about the Shakers, he was a Shaker. He read with perfect empathy: he was Rilke for hours, Camus, Faulkner. I remember an afternoon when he turned into Heraclitus, and through this mask savaged Martin Heidegger. "Heidegger understood nothing of Being." Psellus said that the mind could take any form, but I wonder whether there has ever been as protean an imagination as Thomas Merton's. He could, of an afternoon, dance to Dylan Thomas on a Louisville jukebox, argue an hour later with James Laughlin about surrealism in Latin American poetry, say his offices in an automobile headed back to Gethsemani, and spend the evening writing to a mullah in Pakistan about techniques of meditation.

Gene photographed Tom with a firm realization that he was photographing a

Kierkegaard who was a fan of *Mad*; a Zen adept and hermit who drooled over hospital nurses with a cute behind and well-turned ankle, and could moreover sweep such a nurse off her feet; a man of accomplished self-discipline who sometimes acted like a ten-year-old with an unlimited charge account at a candy store.

It must be put on record that both Gene and Tom were as stubborn as mules. They knew their minds, as genius always does, and when they went headstrong into an enterprise, nothing could stop them. Both were stoically indifferent to their ailing bodies. They enjoyed having difficult and untenable prejudices. Gene hated television and the movies, color photography ("just some chemicals in the emulsion, nothing to do with photography"), and especially color slides of paintings. I had lots of these, both as teaching aids and for my delight. Gene would sit patiently through a new box of slides if he turned up when Bonnie Jean and I were having an evening of projecting.

"Oh, Lord!" Gene would say. "This man can't draw worth a damn."

"Gene, this is Rembrandt." (Or Caravaggio, or Degas.)

"I don't care who he is. The human leg can't bend that way."

When he brought his photographs over to show, always mounted, he was modestly silent. We did the talking, not he. He talked only about others' photographs. I like to think that Gene's final suite of photographs—of Kentucky trees winter bare, made Cézanne-like by kicking the tripod—was a continuation of the Merton photographs, for they were of Tom's favorite place, the Kentucky woods. His cabin was remoter than Thoreau's, and he was there for twenty-seven years more than Thoreau lived at Walden. They were both men suspicious of man's wisdom but in awe of, and in search of, God's.

The last time Gene and I were present with Tom was with Tom's spirit only. We were at dinner at Tommie O'Callaghan's home in Louisville. She was Tom's devoted patron, typist, and go-between with the world. John Howard Griffin was there also. Tommie was one of the few people who had demanded, and been allowed to see,

Tom's body in its U.S. Air Force coffin. She had not been able to recognize him, so severe was the facial distortion. Tom, who noticed everything, and who knew more about the world than forty other people together, had not noticed a frayed electrical cord to his fan in Bangkok and had not known that the East has direct current rather than alternating. In *Cables to the Ace* he had written:

> Oh the blue electric palaces of polar night
> Where the radiograms of hymnody
> Get lost in the fan!

And Gene called me one Sunday morning to say that he'd had a dream about Tom. He was getting off an old-fashioned electric trolley in some Eastern city (turbans, robes) and its trolley pole had fallen and hurt him. A few days later Gene called to say he'd heard of Tom's death by electrocution in Bangkok.

Early summer 1967, my home

PHOTOGRAPHING THOMAS MERTON: A REMINISCENCE

by Ralph Eugene Meatyard

It was a blustery mid-winter day. Three of us, Jonathan Williams, poet/publisher; Guy Davenport, poet/scholar; and myself had gone to visit Thomas Merton. Jonathan had corresponded with him about producing a book.

I had read some of his books, or papers, or poems, I didn't remember which. I remember that I had liked what I had read. I didn't ever recall having seen a picture of him—but from the first moment a group of monks had come out of the building to meet us, I knew which one was Tom. We hit it off famously from the first. Our interests were all the same, some more avidly in one area, some another.

It was noontime. Tom asked if we had eaten. We had not. Tom wondered if we would rather go to a restaurant or to his cabin for a simple lunch of cheese and bread. We went to his place. I thought that I had never enjoyed myself so much over a lunch in my entire life. Sharp Trappist cheese, the no-longer-available Trappist goat cheese (dry and crumbly and fantastic), Trappist-made butter, Trappist-made bread (solid and perfectly wedded), and a good drink—this was our entire meal. Lunch lasted for about four hours as we slowly, satisfyingly filled our bellies. Our heads were filled with equally delicious talk about people, places, things—literary, religious, political. I made photographs of Tom with meal and books (he was dressed like a stevedore and reminded me of the look of Picasso)—of Tom reading from what proved to be *Cables to the Ace* (at that time notes, and later called "Edifying Cables").

Permission to publish this essay was kindly given by Christopher Meatyard.

The change in title was prophetic. I believe that Tom took hold of his cable to the Ace in Bangkok.

Late in the afternoon we took our leave of Tom and he loaded us down with whole wheat bread and more cheese. I never expected to enjoy myself as much again. Fortunately I was wrong. There were many more meetings and good times with my "especial Uncle" Tom.

Through means of the pictures that I had made, I next met one of the greatest families in Louisville, Frank and Tommie O'Callaghan. Tommie is the executor of Tom's estate and their house was a home base for him while he was in Louisville.

In May, she asked if I would like to attend the ordination services for Dan Walsh, in which Tom was to take part. Dan had been Tom's mentor while in college and had talked Tom into joining the monastery—now Tom had talked Dan into becoming a priest.

It was at this ordination that I was to get to know Tom's religious side as well as his literary. I had never before attended a high Catholic ceremony. The day promised to be long, and the dreary weather and rain to make it even more so. The beautiful robes, the involved movings and posturings, the extreme age of the archbishop and especially the evident highly emotional state of the ordainee all made a magnificent panorama.

It is written that a Mass is celebrated—but I doubt if ever as expansively, as reverently, as tremendously as Tom was able to do on this day. Tom ate of the body/ wafer and I do mean *ate*. He drank of the blood/wine and I do mean *drank*. He opened wide his arms over the kneeling figure of his friend Dan—for the first time that day the sun shone; shone down through the skylight and onto the figures of Tom Merton and Dan Walsh—there was room enough in the outstretched arms to encompass the entire universe. Everyone in the audience was moved beyond belief.

That afternoon at a buffet for Father Dan I gave him a portrait that I had made of Tom. He said that it was one of his finest gifts. We spent several hours visiting with friends, eating and drinking. Most of the time Tom and I were visiting at a large, round table with five of his students, all ex-novices, some with wives. At this time I learned of the desires, frustrations, dreams and needs of those who commit themselves for as long as eight years and then, finally, decide that the monastery life is not for them.

A picnic early that summer had many memorable individual events. Tom met us wearing a fishing cap with an emblem of crossed swordfish. We saw one or two other monks wearing them also. It seems that some man had purchased a group of items at a sale of sporting goods and subsequently donated the caps to the Trappists. They all were wearing them to work in. We had much nice food on the edge of a field where Joan Baez had played and sung for Tom the week before, and the picture he evoked of her running down the hill with her hair flying wildly behind her was indicative of the talk and mood for the entire day.

A few of the people had to go back early to Louisville, and we retired to an unused farmhouse and farmyard where I proceeded to make some photographs of Tom and Guy. Backgrounds are important to my photographs and I used many around that farm for constructions and single and double portraits. There was one junction of a row of large leafed plants, a gate going to nowhere and a plowed field that looked interesting. I asked Tom to walk along next to the plants while I worked the camera. As he was walking he asked how far to go and I said for him to keep going. He did—and disappeared from view in the ground glass. I looked up and he was lying on his face in the field with his hat on his head. He was participating. None of us realized that there was a nine-inch drop-off from grass to field. We all laughed until we could laugh no longer—a pratfall is contagious in its humor.

When we recovered I made more photos of Guy and Tom with a tub of mosquito larvae; with them by the house; the barn with Tom looking like a real live old-world monk and like one who had just returned as a prodigal to the old homestead. We took Tom back to the monastery and we departed for home.

I remember days in Lexington, talks about Zen and Sufism, about the role of the Church in the world, about genocide, the Civil War in America and the current scene of suicides and riots. I remember talks with a *Life* magazine writer and an Oxford don. More meetings with the same people and with Wendell Berry and with Denise Levertov; I remember talks about Parra and Lax, Zukofsky and Patchen, Paul Metcalf and James Laughlin, Camus and Joyce. I remember talks about places—India, our Indian lands, Africa and Monte Albán. I remember hopes for *Cables to the Ace* and *The Geography of Lograire*. I remember Monks Pond and his saying that it had frozen over in his last issue of it—and I remember Tom saying that in Life if you are too intent on winning you will never enjoy playing. I am trying to enjoy living and playing in life as he did.

Early summer 1967, picnic on edge of woods

Early summer 1967, roaming on abandoned farm near monastery

A EULOGY OF THOMAS MERTON

by Ralph Eugene Meatyard

I am a Protestant. Father Louis, Thomas Merton, was closer to God than anyone I ever met in my life. He exuded goodness and graciousness. He was not a holier-than-thou religious person. He was not out of this world, but very much with it.

I met Tom three years ago and spent quite a bit of time with him. He enjoyed my photos and I enjoyed his talk. He was not a communist hippie left-leaning sympathizer, nor was he of the right. He saw a problem from all sides.

I found Tom's writings at times somewhat in the difficult-to-understand region—his talk never obscure. He loved to eat and a picnic of a fondue or a quiche and wine was something he appreciated immensely.

The last time I saw Tom was two days before he left for India. We dined for a long time over curry and talked about all the great times we had had recently, laughed over a pratfall he took while participating in one of my pictures. We listened to his favorite records while he played the bongos. He showed me his new camera. Uncle Tom—as my children called him—gave my daughter Melissa his collection of his favorite publication—*Mad* magazine. We said good trips to each other—and I had a feeling that I would never see him again.

I had my last letter from him three days ago. He had had several nice meetings with the Dalai Lama and his monks in the Himalayas; he had enjoyed them thoroughly and was looking forward to spending Christmas in Java. I am sure that the DC that took Tom (he was accidentally electrocuted by a fan with faulty wiring)

This eulogy was published in *The Kentucky Kernel*, December 13, 1960.

was just that—direct. He was unable to cope with the outside world. He was perhaps the only person in the world naive enough to grab a live electric wire.

Tom this past summer was re-examining Camus, Joyce, Blake and concrete poetry. His favorite of his own books was *The Way of Chuang Tzu*. I think his best was *Cables to the Ace*. I hope Tom spreads Mars bars (his name for the good things of the material world, especially a drink with friends, which his poverty denied him) from one end of Heaven to the other. If such a place deserves to exist, it deserves it for Tom Merton to be free in.

Midsummer picnic, 1967

CORRESPONDENCE

between Thomas Merton and
Ralph Eugene Meatyard

eight twelve sixty seven

Dear Tom—

Returned just this week from 3½ wks vacation & travel through the East & North. Went to Bloomington, Ind.; Urbana, Ill.; Bloomington, Ill.; Chicago, Cleveland, Buffalo, Rochester, Boston, Storrs, Conn.; NYC, Philadelphia, Columbus, O.; & home. We saw many people & bought lots of books.

While I was away the good people at the Speed [Museum in Louisville] thought it would be nice to hang my pictures in the hallway for two weeks, so they did. Because of that & no one knowing of it, CJ [Louisville *Courier-Journal*] decided not to use article & pictures by me in Sunday magazine—no useful connection they said—so next in that area is Bellarmine.

I'm hard at work on getting the new store opened & in operation. Would it be possible to see you on Monday, Labor Day? Bring family for picnic? Bring only Guy [Davenport] & maybe Wendell Berry or Jonathan Greene?—Just always nice to see you!

Made many more pictures while away, & by first of year should have around a 1000 negatives to print.

Would you be willing to try something in an experimental vein? If not just say so & it will be perfectly all right with me & I will understand. What I propose is to see how closely I, or any artist can connect with the utterances of another. If you were to send me words, prose or poetry & number of words doesn't matter & I don't necessarily understand the personal or private meaning of them—then try to make a photograph or pigraphs of them! We might also if that works try my abstracted photo first & then your words.

Many things to tell you when I see you again, until then—

Love,
Sincerely,
Gene

P.S. I think that I showed you 12 photos of boy along a changing wall each photo with a different mask! Long after making these photos & while thinking of poetic structure I composed this 30 syllable haiku. I don't think that it is too awfully bad for a primitive photo poet!

However,
    Hoover;
        However—
How rove wearer,
    wherever
   lovers rave,
      the prover
of history's hysterical plover.
       —Rem

Aug 15, Trappist Ky.

Dear Gene:

It was good to get your letter, to know that you had had a good vacation, that the new store was taking shape, etc. But I am sorry they made such a secret out of the Speed show. Hope the Bellarmine one will be better and that the CJ coverage will work out.

And maybe even Tommy O'Callaghan's party, if she is not having twins at that time.

I will be happy to see you on Labor Day. Work it either way you like. Probably best to combine it by bringing poets and Madeleine—we could work one for the kids later. Kids have no dearth of picnics. The best time for me would be 11.30 standard time. That is about when you came last time. So unless I hear different I'll expect you 11.30 laborday.

I like very much your suggestion of trying something experimental; poems and pictures. Let's think about that. But first of all, I need a cover for my new book, Edifying Cables. Some of those we looked at last time would be great. Maybe I'll send you the text however and you can look it over and see if it gives you any special ideas.

Lately I got out the local Rolleiflex and tried some more roots and other strange shots. But there is no one here interested in doing a decent job of processing. Do you know anyone who could be trusted to do a good job, especially in bringing out what needs to be brought out in some of those root shapes and textures? I don't want to send the stuff to a straight commercial shop. If you can recommend someone, I'll be happy. The fellow who did such good work for me before has gone to the monastery in South America.

Looking forward to seeing you Laborday,

all my best,
Tom

nine ten sixty seven

Dear Tom—

Thanks so much for time last, most edifying. We were at Guys saturday & he is still somewhat tensed.

I imagine that you have heard from Jon'than Wms. re his tour. He mentions in letter to me to try to arrange tour to you on Saturday afternoon, the 21st October. I have to work 'til 1 P.M. & wonder if Sunday 22nd is alright with you if it is with him. Guy acts like he would back out in any case. Let me know soon on this.

Bellarmine week is Nov 5th–12th. I am writing Tommy tonight about that occasion. Could I have 5 or 6 more of your calligraphic drawings to mount & use on my store's walls.

Melissa Meatyard wrote the following poem the first week of school—no help:

> The king skyscraper
> rules the little building
> in his kingdom.
>
> Because he is the king
> of the buildings in
> his kingdom.
>
> The lonely king
> skyscraper shakes when
> we have snow.

Today we went gathering bittersweet, buckeyes, & made tomato relish & chutney.

Love,
Gene

Sept 11, 1967

Dear Gene:

I was expecting my publisher this weekend and hoping we might look over the photos and also even get over to Lexington. Well, he didn't show. He had to go to Montreal to look after Ezra Pound who unpredictably came to Expo for a poet festival of some sort. I am sending the photos to him with my suggestions and we'll see how he reacts.

It didn't dawn on me what the precise subject of the exhibit at Bellarmine was going to be. Tommie O'Callaghan informed me. That's sort of overwhelming, but fine. Especially because it means not waiting to February to see the photos. The only thing I'd say would be: be sure not to have any obvious picnic photos in there, because of the local taboo.

It was good to have you all here the other day and I very much enjoyed it.

Here are some of the recent follies and fables. They might interest you, here and there.

My best to all of you,
Tom

[n.d.]

Dear Gene

Here are some artifacts. Pick the ones you want—and as for the others—what do you think? If you can get any buyers at $15 @ will split the takings, and I can use the fortune in my Mars bar fund.

I think Sunday 22 Oct. will be ok as I am trying to get out of giving lectures on Sunday for a while. Maybe I could see the Bellarmine pix then, in case I can't get in to B.?

Best to all of you
Tom

I liked Melissa's Building Poem—Lewis Mumford would agree.

Wednesday 18 [October 1967]

Dear Gene:

This is just to confirm that I am expecting you Sunday 22, at about 11.15 or 11.30, right? You said there was doubt about coming Saturday—but Jonathan wrote he was coming Saturday. So far, with me, it's Sunday?

Let me know by mail if there is any change. Best. Hope we have nice weather. Am looking forward.

as ever
Tom

June 23 1968

Dear Gene:

I've been one very busy and overvisited monk lately and I must admit I totally forgot about the exhibit of mss and drawings. You have drawings I think (I don't have much around now). I am sending herewith some mss and other bits and pieces. Among these items are a large number of copies of the Macaronic Antipoem. We might sell them 5 cents a piece for some worthy cause (would it be too much trouble to keep track?) like the Catholic Peace Fellowship.

I'll send extra batch of macaronics in another envelope.

It would be nice if I could sneak over and see it. Right now I am getting ready to go into retreat for the month of July and catch up on the meditation etc. It has been a whirl (for me) the last couple of months. Lax was here but the only available days were during the week so I didn't even try to contact you about getting over. We were busy all the time anyhow. Tommie came out with all her kids and it was very hot too. I was in a daze. Her mother just died by the way.

Took a pile of fine pix out in California but they aren't all processed yet in fact I haven't even seen contacts of most of them. The place where I was was superb, very wild and isolated. Also New Mexico briefly on the way back. Wonderful desert rocks.

Hope to get together with you in August sometime. Will write again later when I have soaked up a little more silence.

My best always,
Tom

July 29, 1968

Dear Gene:

Very good to hear from you again. Glad to hear of creativity and development in all fields including viniculture. And I'm glad to hear about the possible exhibit in Sept. I'll get over for it if I can but can't guarantee anything.

However, if you can get over one of these weekends, let's get together for a sandwich al fresco. Hoping for some fresco weather and not just the kind of general steam heat we've got now. Any time like weekend of Aug 18th or thereafter but Sept 7th is booked up. If you prefer Sunday that's ok. Name the day and I'll meet you at gate about 12. OK??

Monks Pond iii slowly coming on with a poem by Chris. I've put him in authors' notes as being 12 yrs old. Please let me know if he has now added another birthday—or if I was wrong from the start.

> Best to you and Midi and all,
> Cordially,
> Tom

Wednesday [May 29, 1968]

Dear Gene:

Just a hasty note in answer to your letter, which I got yesterday when I returned from California and New Mexico. It was a really great trip and I enjoyed every minute of it. Hope to talk about it with you.

Sunday is unfortunately impossible. I am going to be tied up with a conference with some nuns. The next week or two will be very crowded. I don't think I can plan on anything until about mid-June. I still don't know when Lax wants to come, but I'll get in touch as soon as I find out.

My best to you and Madeleine. Thanks too for Chris's great poem. I'll fit it in to the pond, when I get around to working on two and three. Ran into poets in San Francisco and in fact slept on the floor of the office of City Lights Publications. (There was a matress). North Beach section really great.

Best always,
Tom

6-17-68

Dear Tom—

Thanks for nice issue of Monks Pond—looks real great! Assume that you have been working mightily. Wendell [Berry] & I have been doing much much on first part of Red River book with many trips to various parts of the gorge.

Do you yet remember my asking if it would be possible to put on a show here of some of your pictures & manuscripts—? Would like this for August–September.

Will be nice to see you again.

Gene

June 29 [1968]

Dear Gene

Here's another possibility for your exhibit. A concrete poem. Might be mounted? I leave you to judge.

When it is turned upside down you get it in an instant Greek translation.

Best
Tom

OVID   DIVO
VOID   DIOV

```
IDOV    IOVD
VIDO    OVID

VOID    DIOV
DVOI    OIVD
IDVO    OVID
OIDV    VOID

IVOD    DOVI
VIDO    OVID
OVID    VIDO
DOVI    IVOD

DVOI    VOID
IDVO    VIDO
OIDV    IDOV
VOID    DIVO
```

Aug 15, 1968

Dear Gene:

I am very sorry to have to change the signals. It is necessary for me to go to Washington on the weekend of the 23–25th, and I won't be able to keep our picnic date for the 25th. I am still free on Sept. 1 myself, if that is still open for you all—or maybe I would be able to drop over during the following week. I can get transportation fairly easily right now.

My plans for Asia are shaping up and it seems I will be busy out there and meet quite a few interesting people of all religions. I look forward to it greatly.

With my warm regards, as ever,
Tom

I'm using another of Chris's poems in MPOND IV.

Thursday, Sept 5 [1968]

Dear Gene

I seem to remember you said something about a pair of glasses? I guess I could use an extra pair—I'm bad at losing things and I don't especially like the frames of the ones I have anyhow. What do you think would be better? Darker frames? Anyway, I got the prescription.

I'm taking off early next week to see the Apaches dancing in New Mexico—so you'd have to *mail* the glasses. Is that safe? I guess so.

Best address, until Sept 30—

c/o W H Ferry
Box 4068
Santa Barbara, Cal.
93103

Naturally I'm most grateful.

Certainly enjoyed your visit—am still working on the remnants!

Keep well—I'll be in touch with you all.

Best wishes—Peace—Joy
Tom

[September 21, 1968]

Dear Gene

Alaska is fantastic. Indian–Russian–Orthodox village up the road from where I am. In most places—not even roads. You fly in & out!

Best to all of you
Tom Merton

San Francisco [October 5, 1968]

Dear Gene

When I got to Santa Barbara two days ago the glasses were there—they are really fine & I am most grateful. Having a fine time in Cal. This motel is incredible, wild camp! You must see it some day.

Tom

Nov 28. 68.

Dear Gene

Thanks for yours of the 6th—forwarded to me in Calcutta while I was up in the Himalayas. Saw the Dalai & a flock of other Lamas & had some great talks with them. Real disciplined meditation outfits they have! After about a month with Tibetans here & there I've come south—like it a lot, wish I had more time here—off to Ceylon this afternoon, then Bangkok. I'll be in Bangkok until Dec 15. Address.
AIM Meeting
c/o Missions Estrangères de Paris
254 SILOM Rd.
Bangkok, Thailand
After that I'll be at a monastery in Indonesia until right after Xmas—
Pertapaan Cist.
Rawa Seneng
Temanggung
Java
Indonesia
After that I don't know for sure. Anything is possible as long as the money doesn't give out.

I hope the Niles' show was successful—glad to hear all about the one at Eyeglasses!

Love to all, Merry Christmas in case I don't get a chance to write fast again.

Tom

Picnic, fall 1967

Tom as farmer holds thyrsus of Jonathan Williams, fall 1967

Tom and Baptist sweatshirt, late fall 1967

A NOTE

by Christopher Meatyard

Between January 18, 1967, and September 1, 1968, Ralph Eugene Meatyard took 116 photographs of Father Louis—Thomas Merton—mostly in the vicinity of the monastery of Gethsemani at Bardstown, Kentucky. Thomas Merton was a subject who carefully articulated his life around the terms of a singular idea. He gave up his personal possessions, his heritage, and his freedom to assume the identity (the iconological mask) of the Cistercian Order of the Strict Observance, the Trappists. Merton's "mask" was not so different from anyone else's, although it was more clearly defined by the traditions and iconography of the Catholic Church. It was from this perspective that Merton began to reach out in his last years, valuing the diversity of human relations and human freedom as a revelation of his creator's unqualified love. But he could not vividly know that freedom except by degrees of contrast to his own "masked" vigil. While most of Meatyard's work is abstract and characterized by an emotionally charged formalism, nowhere is it more justifiably narrative than in his portraits of Thomas Merton.

Gene's camera, after years of reliable service, was beginning to show minor symptoms of its age. On several occasions the back of the camera let in light, which shows up as unexpected flares on the images. Every so often the film-advance

The observations above are based on a careful examination of the negatives. The reconstruction of photographic sequences is in accordance with the edge numbers of the negatives. Objects and situations in the prints were identified with the aid of Guy Davenport, Brother Patrick Hart, and Madelyn Meatyard. Additional recollection of events was generously provided by Robert Daggy, Carolyn Hammer, Tommie O'Callaghan, and Robert Shepherd.

mechanism moved unevenly; as a result, some frames overlapped slightly (and not deliberately, as with a multiple exposure), others were spaced too far apart, and often the last image was not on the roll. Frequently the irregularities were fortuitous, as when Gene photographed Merton on the occasion of a summer picnic (pages 46 and 47) and a blank space appeared in an otherwise full roll of twelve frames. Merton, wearing his fishing cap and monk's habit, was directed to walk away from the camera to where, without warning, the ground dropped nine inches to a plowed field. Blind to the drop, Merton asked, "How far?" and Gene answered, "Keep going." Merton's stride found the vertical and he fell facedown, his robes billowing and flashing all of him there was to see to those assembled, including at least two women. I suppose my father intended for Merton to hop that step so that he could suspend him softly, airborne, and momentarily relate the monk to the ephermeral windswept wire with its solitary clothespin that reached toward him from the top of the inexplicable gatepost frame. (Wires, cables, and power lines were an important formal element in all the photographs made that day.) In the next frame Merton is seen marching back toward the camera, grinning broadly. Although one of Gene's passions was recording the interstice of gesture—and he would not have let this moment pass—in this case the frame is blank for the fall itself, the record discrete. Gene dated the photograph "fall" even though the picnic took place in the early summer.

Meatyard, in the company of Guy Davenport and Jonathan Williams, first met Merton on January 18, 1967, at the hermitage that the monastery had built to allow him more solitude. There were no steps, so the guests hoisted themselves up one and a half feet to the front porch. From inside the cabin, the windows, lacking vertical mullions, looked like ladders ascending to the sky. Through them one could see the rolling pastures almost all the way to New Hope. The cabin offered an abundance of chairs made with Shaker simplicity by nuns. The only structural embellishment to the concrete-block and slab-floor hermitage was a fieldstone fireplace with a cross laid into it in high relief. Merton kept a wood fragment from the top of the abbot's old chair resting on the mantel like a clock, saved by its embossed cross from numerous possible stokings of the fire in the hearth below. Greek icons, gifts from friends such as Marco Pallis and Bob Rambuch, hung on the walls.

The first photographs of Merton were made around a flat pine-top worktable spread with the remains of lunch. We can see slices of bread, cheese, a tin of fruitcake, all products of the Trappists at Gethsemani (pages 12–13). Merton leaned one elbow on his slant-top writing desk. Writing was his form of monastic labor. Immediately before Merton is a two-handled mug: the monks held these with both hands to concentrate on the act of drinking and remember their adopted childlike innocence.

Meatyard took eight pictures of Merton sitting at the table. Five were focused exclusively on the books; Merton and the table of food were left in soft focus. One negative concentrated strictly on the food. Of the two remaining negatives, which were actually focused on Merton, one, a multiple exposure, transliterates the scene into an interplay of visual textures.

In four more views from a slightly different angle, Meatyard highlighted Merton's head with a crescent of light (pages 14–15). He isolated the singular volume and contrasted it against the flatness of wall, window, and icons. In front, the flat silhouette of Davenport's head closed the sandwich of planes.

Meatyard made nine images of Merton's profile as he read from the manuscript that would become *Cables to the Ace* (pages 2, 16–19). Each explored a different relationship between the silhouette and the outlining illumination. Meatyard modified Merton's location by degrees to draw attention to the juxtaposition of the horizontal frame of the window and the vertical support post of the porch outside. He illustrated Merton's apophatic speech by aligning one black arm of the momentary crucifix with the speaker's ebullient tongue.

After this session indoors, the four men put on jackets and coats and went for a walk. When they came to the sheep barn, Meatyard made six more photographs of

Merton (pages 20–22); these concluded his day's work. Kentucky skies are often overcast, with the light mottled through clouds, and the first two negatives are softer in contrast than the subsequent four. With thicker clouds the light was more widely scattered. In the first two photographs Merton has his eyes pinched tight by his brow. Only in these two can we see, barely, the rafters through the window as they recede into the darkness of the barn's interior. Merton had a white notepad tucked into the waist pocket of his denim jacket, and a note on the print reminds us that this place was one of his favorite spots: "Many poems written here." The next two negatives depict Merton moving his head from side to side, and the last two show him looking up. The directional lines of his head moving back and forth and up and down form an image of central significance for Merton: the penitential cross, which he internalized daily in meditation and prayer.

In all the photographs, Meatyard sought to make visible some significant connection between Merton and his environment, and he paid special attention to even the least obvious, but nevertheless tangible, relationships of light and form. He observed details that we might discard as random coincidence, then revealed these details as pointed integrally to one subject, at one place, in one moment of time.

Meatyard next saw Merton at the ordination of Dan Walsh and the reception afterward at Tommie O'Callaghan's house in Louisville. No photographs were taken. Instead, on this occasion Meatyard spent his hours absorbing Merton's passionate evocation of monastic ceremony, as well as his candid contributions to a long conversation about the hardships of monastic duty.

On June 24, Merton solicited transporation from his friend Robert Shepherd, a graphic artist and publications director at the University of Kentucky in Lexington. The ailing artist Victor Hammer had requested Merton's presence for the purpose of receiving absolution. After meeting with Hammer, Merton and Shepherd collected Guy Davenport, and the three went to Meatyard's home (pages 37–38). Merton wore denim jeans and a denim shirt with long sleeves rolled up to the elbow; the shirt had white enameled snaps. In his shirt pocket were a pen and an eyeglass case. He wore the eyeglasses to look at some photographs, which can be seen reflected in the lenses. Meatyard made at least three dozen photographs that day and destroyed more than half of them. (It was uncommon for him to edit negatives, but from the discontinuity of the edge numbers it appears likely that he did so in this instance.) Most of the surviving negatives concentrate on Merton's reactions to the conversation. None shows Merton drinking, although he frequently has a glass prominently in hand.

At Gethsemani in the early summer of 1967, Tommie O'Callaghan catered a large picnic on the edge of some woods (pages 43–56). O'Callaghan was six or seven months pregnant. Marie Sharon, who assisted O'Callaghan with the organization of Merton's papers, was present, as were Guy Davenport and Meatyard's wife, Madelyn. Merton wore his monk's habit, and provided Meatyard with his first and best opportunity to photograph him so attired. The black and white elements of the habit represent diverse aspects of the Trappist heritage. The white robe is a reminder of the twelve apostles and of the Trappists' dedication to the Virgin, and is worn in choir. The black scapular dates back to the time of St. Benedict, the sixth century, when it functioned as an apron for those involved in manual labor. The hood of the scapular was seldom used except in processions. The contrast of black and white corresponds to Merton's own personal combination of two branches of theological discourse: the apophatic, referring to the unknowability of God, and the cataphatic, referring to the theology of "light," "good," "life." The wide leather belt "girds up the loins" and thus represents a profession of monastic vows (elsewhere Merton can be seen wearing this belt of profession even on top of another belt looped through jeans). A fishing cap bearing a pair of crossed swordfish as insignia tops off Merton's habit.

After O'Callaghan and Sharon left to complete some business at the monastery, the rest of the group went to an abandoned farm nearby so that Meatyard could take more photographs. These all incorporate as a key motif the graphic lines of cable wire and thus relate to two subjects that had been brought up in the first meeting between Meatyard and Merton. General Electric, the original benefactor of Merton's hermitage, had wanted to build an elaborate U-shaped, glass-walled ecumenical retreat house and conference center. Merton, who usually made pretense to apologize for his humble dwelling, was clearly jubilant about his decision not to let GE build this pavilion. The company's patronage is tied into the poem Merton was writing in his modest hermitage when Meatyard first visited him. The poem, which would be titled *Cables to the Ace*, was then called *Edifying Cables*, and it refers often to the plurality of wire messages for communication but none with more resolute spring than the electrical transmission of life into afterlife.

A picnic held in the woods in midsummer brought the Meatyards together with Merton and Wendell and Tanya Berry. Merton wore a short-sleeved denim shirt (pages 59–63). As had not happened on earlier occasions, Meatyard photographed Merton together with the others present. Interspersed among the negatives from this picnic are numerous multiple-exposure compositions that Meatyard made looking up into the tree canopy. He photographed Wendell Berry's head superimposed over Merton's and made multiple exposures of Merton alone. Meatyard spent several years working with multiple exposure, and he used it as the principle style for his nonfigurative views of landscape and architecture. With multiple exposure he could intensify the harmony and the cacophony of rhythm shifting to a fever pitch the controlled coincidence among objects.

The next meeting of Meatyard and Merton took place in late October 1967 (pages 76–81). The photographer was accompanied by Jonathan Williams, Guy Davenport, and Davenport's friend Bonnie Jean Cox. The first photograph Meatyard made that day was a self-portrait. As usual, he had the camera on a tripod, but in this case he stood a few feet down the woodland path in the middle of the field of view and operated the camera with one outstretched arm. He was wearing a suit and tie. During the exposure he made a lateral circular movement and with this gesture gave himself a third eye, on his forehead. Above was an oak leaf that translated white from its autumnal yellow. After one exposure he returned to his position behind the camera. With the leaf and trees as reference, he made two portraits of Merton standing at the edge of the path: in one he looks into the camera, and in the other, toward the fluttering leaf.

The other images from this day introduce a new icon, which Merton adopted with marked enthusiasm. Williams brought along a thyrsus he had commissioned from a woodcraft teacher named Taylor in Penland, North Carolina. The thyrsus, a staff entwined with ivy or grapevines and surmounted by a pine cone, is here an elaborate hybrid of historical prototypes and contemporary innovations. Williams connected the trident of Poseidon with the thyrsus of Dionysius, but an ear of corn forms the middle prong of this thyrsus, thus identifying the bearer as a bacchant of Appalachia, whose modern-day drink was not wine but corn whiskey. In the photographs in which Merton held the thyrsus, Meatyard drew on the fertility connotations of the staff. He photographed Merton in front of an apple orchard with wild persimmon trees and among harvested rows of corn that the monks raised for their livestock. A cornstalk appears as the phallus of Merton's shadow. The two photographs of Merton standing in the cornfield form a pair, but Meatyard emphatically darkened the print in which Merton looked up, to a degree that allows us to assume a veiled reference to the differentiation between apophatic (dark) and cataphatic (light). Merton's shaded side faced the camera; in his right hand he held Davenport's straw hat. In the lighter print the hat is turned to reflect light; in the darker one it is turned to show its full shaded bowl, and that subtle gesture heightens the contrast between the light and dark prints.

On a heavily overcast day in late autumn 1967, Meatyard visited Merton at the hermitage, and he brought with him Madelyn, their children Melissa and Christopher, and his closest photographic colleague from Lexington, Robert May (page 83). Meatyard photographed Merton alone and posed him outside wearing a T-shirt inscribed KATALEGETE, the name of an ecumenical magazine published by Jim Holloway, a professor at Berea College and a friend of Merton's. Several of the variations from this short session were multiple exposures, which generate a visual tension with the word KATALEGETE. May took candid photographs of Meatyard at work, as well as of the entire group returning to the hermitage. (Meatyard, it should be noted, never took any family snapshots or made casual records after 1955.)

In late December 1967, Wendell and Tanya Berry, Denise Levertov, and Madelyn and Gene Meatyard met again with Merton at the hermitage (pages 95–99). Meatyard photographed the poets—Merton, Levertov, and Berry—in two sessions, the first inside the hermitage with the three sitting around the fireplace, and the second outside, where they gathered around an old rusting wheelbarrow. Merton wore a hip-length field jacket over his denim work clothes, his jeans rolled up around his ankles. In several photographs he seems to be emphasizing his words by placing his left hand on top of his head; the movement lifts his shirt so that its white enameled snaps repeat themselves in triplicate. Levertov slices the air with open palm and fingers; Berry clasps a thin volume with both hands and appears more still.

Berry, who is reading from the book, offers a concrete visual reference to the idea of poetry, so Meatyard aligned his perspective with him. Meatyard has often been described as having been unobtrusive while he photographed and part of this is due to the camera itself. His Rolleiflex angled light upward, with a mirror projecting the vista into a six-centimeter-square viewing field in the top of the camera; he bent his head forward in order to see the image. There is quite a difference between this and a thirty-five-millimeter camera held like a mask in front of the photographer's face, while the subject is self-consciously aware of being scrutinized and recorded. The medium-format Rolleiflex is less dominant and less obtrusive: the camera allows the acute presence of the photographer to fade, his head tipped down as though browsing through a book.

It was at this December meeting that Levertov and Merton discussed the merits of self-immolation as a way of protesting the war in Vietnam. It is tempting to see a visual commentary on this conversation in the triple exposure with the overlapping visages of Levertov, Merton, and Berry: almost every one of its overlapping forms refers to fire. Levertov is seated in front of an active fireplace. The vivid wood grain of the cedar altar over the hearth opening recalls flames. Another image of the altar is superimposed in that of the gas heater. The horizontal exhaust of the heater intersects with the altar candle. The candle snuff reflects a flamelike light. A second image of the altar candle hovers under a thermometer, which blends together with an altar icon.

Outside the hermitage Meatyard made another statement, a strangely conjunctive visual addition to the verbal conversation. Meatyard posed the poets around an old wheelbarrow that the monks had used when building the hermitage; Merton had used the same wheelbarrow to haul young trees to replace the older ones lost during the construction. Meatyard softened the focus around the feet of the trio and placed Merton and Levertov behind the wheelbarrow, thus making them seem as if they had been dug up like trees and loaded there. The next photograph completes the episodic transplantation of young poets in front of several of Merton's transplanted trees visible in the background. The small group of photographs made around the wheelbarrow was blithely conceived. Once the subjects were in place the photographer had to act quickly to keep the mood light and avoid the formal rigidity of a pose. There is almost a cinematic quickness, and more than in any of the other photographs, Meatyard's presence is felt here as a result of the strange hyperopic insistence of focus on the distant horizon. The logical extension of focusing on the distant horizon makes the photographer the least focused element, a formless object that is nevertheless the gathering point for the group's attention. Meatyard used focus as a means to refer to himself and humbly included himself with the group portrait. He is the gardener planting seeds for a later harvest.

Merton and Meatyard did not meet again for almost eight months. Merton, having won pronounced freedom from his monastic restrictions, had begun traveling extensively and developing new projects. Meatyard spent much of this time photographing the Red River Gorge in eastern Kentucky for the book *The Unforeseen Wilderness*, a collaboration with Wendell Berry. The last meeting between Meatyard and Merton, on September 1, 1968, took place just before Merton left for the Far East (pages 101–105). Meatyard again brought Madelyn, Melissa, and Christopher. Merton was wearing his robes and was scheduled to say mass; the meeting was thus more brief than usual. He played the bongos, accompanying a jazz record. At the right-hand edge of one of the photographs Meatyard took, a pile of Merton's calligraphic drawings sits on the pine-top worktable. Meatyard took three photographs of Merton playing the bongos; for one of these Melissa leaned into the camera dancing. As the Meatyards were leaving, Merton asked the photographer to show him how to use the camera John Howard Griffen had sent him. Merton planned to take it along on his long journey to the East; he called it his "Zen camera."

Late fall 1967, Wendell Berry, Tom, Denise Levertov

Playing bongos, early fall 1968, just before trip

Tom, 1968, last picture

Meatyard by Merton, 1968

The text of this book is set in Goudy Old Style, designed in
1915 for American Type Founders by Frederic William Goudy.
The best known American designer of type, Goudy designed over
one hundred typefaces. Goudy Old Style has the smoothness and
evenness of color and generous width of curves that are found
in the designer's best typefaces. It has had a strong influence
on type style in American periodicals and advertising.

Design by Hermann Strohbach
Copyediting by Anna Jardine
Typesetting by Pica Graphics, Monsey, New York
Duotone printing and binding by
South China Printing Company, Hong Kong